Doogle McFrugal

DOOGLE'S HIGHLAND GAMES

Published in association with
Bear With Us Productions

ISBN: 9781739232023

Design by Emma Evans
Illustrated by Andri Anto
www.justbearwithus.com

Written by Tim Fenton

Doogle McFrugal

DOOGLE'S HIGHLAND GAMES

Illustrated by Andri Anto

"This time, Jock," says Doogle

To his faithful little pup,

"I'm going to win a trophy,

A medal or a cup!"

Doogle queues up

For the annual Highland Games.

But he's just an amateur

Against very famous names.

He's been turning up for forty years,

And never won a prize,

Which makes him a winner

In many people's eyes.

He starts with wrestling
Against mighty William Tait.
"I don't have the height!
And I cannot match his weight!"

He's thrown around the field,

Like a child's rag doll.

"Will I ever win?

I'm not doing well at all!"

He can't throw the hammer —

He's dizzy spinning round.

He's third in the hurdles

But... trips and hits the ground!

Now time for cycling,

It's Doogle's best event.

"This will be my year
To enter the winner's tent."

Off to a flying start,

He's soon overtaken

By young, fitter athletes...

His chances forsaken!

At a tricky bend ahead,

Some cyclists crash in a pile.

Doogle takes the lead

For the last quarter of a mile.

Just yards from the finish line,

He can almost touch that medal,

His sporran slips from under him,

Tangling in his pedal!

Up and over the handlebars,
It's not a pretty sight.
"I'm not finished yet!" he yells.
"Not without a fight!"

Back tyre bursts and shreds,
Front wheel bends and buckles.
The crowd all laugh at him,
But he just waves and chuckles.

Once again Doogle's failed,
Other bikes whizz by.

"I won't be beat," he says.
"I'll give it one more try."

Picking up his bike he runs,
'though not very fast,
Carries it over the line —
He hasn't come last!

It's now time for lunch,
There's a break in the events.
Everyone is heading
For the refreshment tents.

The Duke and all his guests,
Looking noble and grand,
Have been watching The Games
From inside the old bandstand.

And as they move to leave,

There's an almighty stramash...

The tiled roof caves in

With a thunderous crash!

Timbers have snapped,

The roof's almost collapsed.

The Duke and royal guests

Are well and truly trapped!

There's a gap in the corner,
One pillar is stronger,
But splintered and bent,
It won't hold out much longer.

Doogle, first on the scene,
Quickly holds up the edge,
While the Duke and his guests
Clamber over the ledge.

The last one gets out

Through a gap just two-foot wide.

Then the whole roof comes down with...

Poor Doogle inside!

People begin screaming:

"Doogle's buried alive!"

"There's no way on this Earth

He can ever survive!"

The dust now settles,

There's a huge pile of rubble,

Wee Jock is barking;

He knows Doogle's in trouble.

Doogle lies motionless.

Then a cough, a fart, a splutter.

"Where's my wee dog Jock?"

Are the first words he does utter.

The pair are reunited,

Jock snuggles up tight.

The crowd all applaud.

"Hooray! Doogle is alright!"

The final game's over,

The Duke faces the crowd.

He speaks with emotion,

His message clear and loud.

"Today we honoured the athlete,
The musician and the dancer.
But if we're looking for a hero?
There's only one answer."

"You've competed here for many years,
Without a medal or decoration.
Today you won our hearts and minds,
And all our admiration."

"'Though beaten by athletes,
Who were stronger and faster,
You were very brave indeed
And saved us from disaster."

"You set a fine example
Of courage beyond belief.
And now I declare you named...
Clan McFrugal Chief!"

After a long and weary day
Doogle's tucked up in bed,
With black eyes, missing teeth,
A bandage round his head.

"Today was wonderful,
The memories I will keep."
Next year's Games he dreams of,
As he falls fast asleep.

Doogle's wee house is
Creaking and cracking,
The roof's full of holes
With an old chimney stack in.

The windows are boarded,
The door hanging squinty,
Waiting for fixing
By Hamish McGinty

A three-legged table,
Chairs with no stuffing.
All the time Doogle
Is huffing and puffing.

Doogle McFrugal

The inspirational story of Doog...
Will he give up the peace and t...
Invershoogle for fame and f...

Written by Tim Fenton

Doogle McFrugal

Illustration by Andri Anto

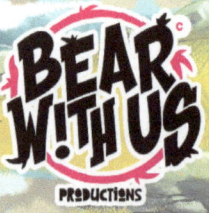